REPORT

Measuring the Performance of the Dallas Police Department

2008–2009 Results

Robert C. Davis

Sponsored by the Communities Foundation of Texas, as administered through the University of North Texas

RAND Center on Quality Policing

A RAND INFRASTRUCTURE, SAFETY, AND ENVIRONMENT CENTER

The research described in this report was sponsored by the Communities Foundation of Texas, as administered through the University of North Texas, and was conducted under the auspices of the RAND Center on Quality Policing within the Safety and Justice Program of RAND Infrastructure, Safety, and Environment (ISE).

Library of Congress Cataloging-in-Publication Data

Davis, Robert C. (Robert Carl)
    Measuring the performance of the Dallas Police Department : 2008-2009 results / Robert C. Davis.
        p. cm.
    Includes bibliographical references.
    ISBN 978-0-8330-4879-0 (pbk. : alk. paper)
    1. Dallas (Tex.). Police Dept.—Evaluation. 2. Police—Texas—Dallas. I. Title.

HV8148.D2D38 2009
363.209764'2812—dc22

                                                                                    2009040658

The RAND Corporation is a nonprofit research organization providing objective analysis and effective solutions that address the challenges facing the public and private sectors around the world. RAND's publications do not necessarily reflect the opinions of its research clients and sponsors.

RAND® is a registered trademark.

© Copyright 2009 RAND Corporation

Permission is given to duplicate this document for personal use only, as long as it is unaltered and complete. Copies may not be duplicated for commercial purposes. Unauthorized posting of RAND documents to a non-RAND Web site is prohibited. RAND documents are protected under copyright law. For information on reprint and linking permissions, please visit the RAND permissions page (http://www.rand.org/publications/permissions.html).

Published 2009 by the RAND Corporation
1776 Main Street, P.O. Box 2138, Santa Monica, CA 90407-2138
1200 South Hayes Street, Arlington, VA 22202-5050
4570 Fifth Avenue, Suite 600, Pittsburgh, PA 15213-2665
RAND URL: http://www.rand.org/
To order RAND documents or to obtain additional information, contact
Distribution Services: Telephone: (310) 451-7002;
Fax: (310) 451-6915; Email: order@rand.org

Preface

This report describes the state of policing in Dallas, Texas, based on the results of four surveys carried out in 2008–2009. The surveys are part of an evaluation of the Caruth Police Institute at Dallas, a partnership of the Dallas Police Department (DPD) with the University of North Texas. The mission of the Caruth Institute, which was founded in January 2009, is to improve the quality of policing in the DPD by promoting staff development, bringing together community and national resources to solve DPD problems, and instituting effective police strategies and practices. This first wave of survey data will act as a benchmark against which to assess the success of the Caruth Police Institute in enhancing the capacity of the DPD to better serve the citizens of Dallas.

Funding for this research was provided by the Communities Foundation of Texas and was administered through the University of North Texas. The Communities Foundation of Texas also funds the Caruth Police Institute.

This report should be of interest to policymakers and community members in Dallas, as well as to persons interested in the Caruth Police Institute and similar efforts to improve the quality of policing.

The RAND Center on Quality Policing

This research was conducted under the auspices of the RAND Center on Quality Policing within the Safety and Justice Program of RAND Infrastructure, Safety, and Environment (ISE). The center conducts research and analysis to improve contemporary police practice and policy. The mission of ISE is to improve the development, operation, use, and protection of society's essential physical assets and natural resources and to enhance the related social assets of safety and security of individuals in transit and in their workplaces and communities. Safety and Justice Program research addresses occupational safety, transportation safety, food safety, and public safety—including violence, policing, corrections, substance abuse, and public integrity.

Copies of surveys described in this report can be obtained by writing to the project leader, Rob Davis, at robert_davis@rand.org. Questions or comments about this report should be sent to the project leader. Information about the Safety and Justice Program is available online (http://www.rand.org/ise/safety), as is information about the Center on Quality Policing (http://cqp.rand.org). Inquiries about research projects should be sent to the following address:

Greg Ridgeway, Director
Safety and Justice Program, ISE
RAND Corporation
1776 Main Street
P.O. Box 2138
Santa Monica, CA 90407-2138
310-393-0411, x7734
Greg_Ridgeway@rand.org

Contents

Figures

Tables

Summary

This report describes the state of policing in Dallas, Texas, based on the results of four surveys carried out in 2008–2009. The surveys included a community survey of randomly selected Dallas residents; a survey of persons who had a recent voluntary or involuntary contact with an officer of the Dallas Police Department (DPD); a survey of police officers to assess job satisfaction, integrity, and perceptions of leadership; and a survey of retail business owners.

The surveys are part of an evaluation of the Caruth Police Institute at Dallas, an initiative to improve the quality of policing in the DPD by promoting staff development, bringing together community and national resources to solve DPD problems, and instituting effective police strategies and practices. The evaluation of the Caruth Institute will examine immediate effects of the institute on developing staff and researching new programs, as well as the global indicators of police services measured, in part, by these surveys. The wave of surveys reported here will act as a benchmark against which to assess the success of the Caruth Police Institute in enhancing the capacity of the DPD to better serve the citizens of Dallas.

The Caruth Police Institute is a partnership of the DPD with the University of North Texas. Both the institute and the evaluation of it are funded by the Communities Foundation of Texas.

Community Opinions of the Police

The community survey was administered to a randomly selected sample of 1,362 Dallas residents between June 25 and November 25, 2008. The survey included sections on police effectiveness, professionalism, fairness, and management. It also included items about neighborhood crime and disorder, as well as victimization. Survey responses were reported for the entire city and also broken down by police division.

Overall, opinions of the police were favorable: Between 70 and 80 percent of respondents expressed positive opinions in response to questions about both police effectiveness and police professionalism. More than 75 percent of Dallas respondents were very or somewhat satisfied with the quality of police services, about 90 percent rated police services as good or better than other city agencies. Only about 20 percent of respondents said that it is common for the police to use excessive force, use offensive language, or break the law or police rules. A larger proportion (roughly one-third) said that it is common for the police to stop people without good reason, and a similar proportion said that the police treat people differently according to gender, ethnic background, religion, or sexual orientation.

Comparisons by division indicated that residents of the Northeast and North Central divisions were more likely to believe that the police are effective, relative to the citywide average. Residents of the Southeast and South Central divisions were less likely than other Dallas residents to rate the police as effective, and residents of the South Central division also rated the police as less professional than other residents did. These differences held even after controlling statistically for effects of age, gender, and race of respondent.

Although there are many problems in making comparisons with other municipalities, Dallas is perceived to be as good or better than other municipalities in which surveys using similar questions have been conducted.

Satisfaction with Police Encounters

Surveys were conducted in early 2009 with 577 persons who had recently reported a property crime and 532 persons who were issued a traffic or Class C summons. The brief surveys measured satisfaction with the way the encounter was handled by the responding police officer(s).

Satisfaction among residents who had a voluntary contact with the police was high. Between 70 and 90 percent of those who had recently called the police to report a victimization were satisfied or very satisfied with how the responding officers handled the incident. Respondents were most satisfied with how respectfully they were treated by the officer(s) and less satisfied with how quickly police responded to the incident. Respondents who had a recent involuntary contact with the police (i.e., received a summons) were somewhat less satisfied with the interaction than residents who had a recent voluntary contact with the police. Still, approximately two-thirds of involuntary-contact respondents were somewhat or very satisfied with all aspects of the encounter.

There were no significant differences between divisions in satisfaction with voluntary police contacts. Residents of one division (South Central) were less satisfied with involuntary contacts than were residents of the other divisions.

Satisfaction rates for Dallas residents who had either a voluntary or involuntary contact with the police were similar to rates for other agencies for which similar surveys have been conducted.

Officer Job Satisfaction, Opinions of Leadership, and Integrity

Web-based surveys were conducted with 688 sworn officers of the DPD in the spring of 2009. The surveys had three parts: questions about job satisfaction, questions about perceptions of leadership in the DPD, and questions about the culture of integrity.

Job satisfaction was mixed. Respondents were most likely to agree that they know what is expected of them on the job (87 percent), that their supervisor cares about them (65 percent), and that their co-workers are committed to doing quality work (64 percent). Officers were least likely to agree that they receive praise for doing good work (30 percent), that their opinions at work count (40 percent), and that someone at work encourages their development (41 percent).

Overall job satisfaction among DPD officers was somewhere between "somewhat satisfied" and "somewhat dissatisfied"—lower than three other law enforcement agencies for which a similar survey was conducted. However, Dallas is the only major city agency among the four.

On items relating to perceptions of leadership in the DPD, there was split in how officers perceived their immediate supervisor and how they perceived leadership at higher levels of the department. Eighty-three percent of DPD officers felt that their immediate supervisor was available to them. However, just one-third or fewer officers believed that departmental leaders communicated to officers what is expected of them (36 percent), were consistent in their expectations (14 percent), articulated a compelling vision of the work of the DPD (25 percent), motivate officers to perform exceptionally (13 percent), or hold themselves to high standards (23 percent).

Dallas officers consistently rated hypothetical ethics infractions as more serious than the average from a national study, suggesting that the DPD has a better than average climate of integrity.

Opinions of the Police Among Retail Business Owners

In December 2008, a mail survey was conducted with owners of retail businesses contained in a database of the Dallas Chamber of Commerce. Twenty-six responses were received. The survey contained seven items, and was modeled after the community survey administered to private citizens described above.

More than 70 percent of respondents gave the DPD a positive rating for crime-fighting effectiveness and working with local businesses. For most other items (prompt response to calls, preventing crimes, maintaining a visible presence, and dealing with problems that concern businesses), the proportion of positive responses fell between 40 and 60 percent.

CHAPTER ONE

Introduction

This interim report summarizes survey data collected in Dallas during 2008–2009. The surveys included

- a community survey to measure public opinion of the Dallas Police Department (DPD)
- contact surveys to assess satisfaction of Dallas citizens with recent police encounters
- officer surveys to gauge job satisfaction, job-related knowledge, perceptions of leadership, and departmental integrity
- surveys of retail business owners to assess satisfaction with police services.

The surveys are part of an evaluation of the Caruth Police Institute at Dallas, a partnership of the DPD with the University of North Texas. The Caruth Institute is intended to improve the quality of policing in Dallas by promoting staff development, bringing together community and national resources to solve DPD problems, and instituting effective police strategies and practices. The institute began in January 2009, and will offer its first classes in police leadership and basic policing skills in the fall of 2009. Both the Caruth Police Institute and the evaluation are funded by the Communities Foundation of Texas.

The evaluation is assessing success of the institute using a variety of methods, including the survey data reported here. The impact evaluation will address changes in a number of domains. We anticipate that these changes will take time to observe, so we believe that the evaluation work should continue at least through the first three years of the institute. Areas in which we plan to assess change include the following:

- **More effective leadership.** One of the direct effects of the institute's leadership training should be a stronger shared vision of effective and respectful policing and enhanced leadership skills. This assessment will come primarily from officer surveys and surveys of Caruth Institute course participants.
- **More effective strategic planning and thinking.** Another direct effect of the institute should be better problem-solving capabilities and a commitment to an evidence-based approach to policing. We will use a variety of methods to assess the extent to which DPD is taking advantage of and benefiting from this aspect of the institute.
- **Enhanced community opinions of the police.** Better police leadership and enhanced problem-solving abilities ought to raise the regard for the department among the public, business leaders, and the media. These outcomes will be assessed through surveys and interviews.

- **Increase in public safety.** The ultimate goal of the institute is to make Dallas a safer place, that is to bring about reductions in crime, fear, and physical and social disorder in targeted areas of city. These measures will be tracked through citizen surveys and examination of DPD crime and nuisance reports.
- **Enhanced DPD influence on national dialogue on policing.** One of the Communities Foundation of Texas's hopes in funding the institute was that it would serve as a model that would influence police agencies across the country. Therefore, an important outcome for the evaluation effort to examine is the extent to which the institute is training officers from other cities and the extent to which DPD becomes a national resource for policing best practices.

This first wave of survey data will act as a benchmark against which to measure any changes in the quality of police services in Dallas that may occur during the upcoming years as a result of the work of the Caruth Institute.

CHAPTER TWO

Measuring Public Trust and Confidence in the Police: The 2008 Dallas Community Survey

Highlights

- More than 75 percent of respondents were very or somewhat satisfied with the quality of police services, and about 90 percent rated police services as good or better than other city agencies.
- One in five Dallas residents believe that it is common for the police to use excessive force, use offensive language, or break the law or police rules. Furthermore, roughly one in three believe that it is common for the police to stop people without good reason, and a similar proportion believe that the police treat people differently according to gender, ethnic background, religion, or sexual orientation.
- Comparisons by division indicated that residents of the Northeast and North Central divisions were more likely to believe that the police are effective, relative to the citywide average. Residents of Southeast and South Central divisions were less likely than other Dallas residents to rate the police as effective, and residents of South Central division also rated the police as less professional than did other residents. These differences held even after controlling statistically for effects of age, gender, and race.
- Although there are many problems in making comparisons with other municipalities, Dallas is perceived to be as good or better than in other municipalities where surveys using similar questions have been conducted.

Introduction

The community survey was conducted by the Schaeffer Center for Public Policy at the University of Baltimore. The Schaeffer Center interviewed 1,362 randomly selected Dallas residents by phone between June 25 and November 25, 2008. The brief survey included questions on opinions of police effectiveness, professionalism, fairness, and management. It also queried Dallas residents about neighborhood crime and disorder problems and victimization. Surveys were completed with 26 percent of households contacted. Details of how the survey was conducted are contained in Appendix A.

In this chapter, we first describe the overall results of the community survey, that is, the totals aggregated across the DPD's seven police divisions. We report the citywide results using data weighted to the population demographics of Dallas. The weighting procedure helps to ensure that the results are less subject to sampling error and more representative of the population make-up of the city. (See Appendix A for a description of the weighting procedure.) Later in this chapter, we compare Dallas's police divisions on individual and composite measures of police effectiveness, police professionalism, and neighborhood problems. Finally, we compare opinions of the police in Dallas to opinions in other municipalities that have used the same survey questions.[1]

Citywide Findings

Opinions of the Police

The first set of questions asked respondents for their opinions about the effectiveness of their neighborhood police. Response options were on a four-point Likert (ordered) scale (e.g., "very good," "somewhat good," "somewhat poor," and "very poor"). The percentages reported below include valid responses to each of the survey questions.

The results for items assessing opinions of police effectiveness are displayed in Figure 2.1. Dallas residents gave the police very high marks for their crime-fighting efforts. Approximately 80 percent of respondents said that the police were doing a somewhat or very good job in combating crime (as opposed to a somewhat or very poor job). The DPD received equally high ratings for its treatment of crime victims: Again, about 80 percent of respondents thought

Figure 2.1
Opinions of Police Effectiveness

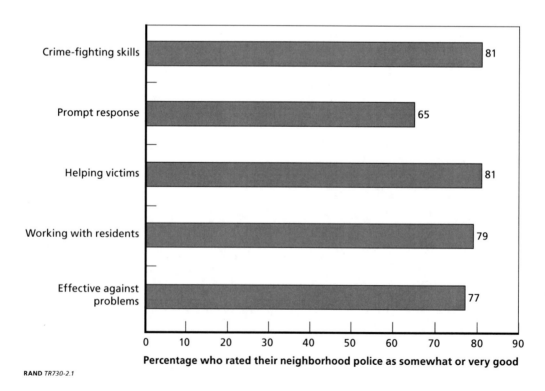

RAND *TR730-2.1*

---

[1]   Weighting the sample results in a minor (approximately 5 percent) reduction in scores on the composite scales of police effectiveness and police professionalism.

that the police in their neighborhood were either somewhat or very helpful toward victims. The DPD was also seen as working constructively to assist residents with problems. Seventy-nine percent of survey respondents believed that the police did a somewhat or very good job of working together with residents to solve local problems, and 77 percent believed that the police were effective in dealing with problems that concern neighborhood residents. Promptness of responding to calls for service was rated somewhat lower: Nearly two-thirds of respondents thought that the DPD responded promptly, but about one-fifth of residents said that the response to calls was not at all prompt.

The next set of items asked questions about police professionalism. Some research findings have suggested that opinions of police professionalism are only somewhat correlated with opinions about police effectiveness.[2] That is, people can think that their local police are effective, but at the same time, believe that they engage in unprofessional behavior. The professionalism items were ranked on a five-point scale, with the following possible responses: "never," "very uncommon," "somewhat uncommon," "somewhat common," "very common," and "don't know."[3]

By each measure we used, a minority of respondents answered the misconduct items affirmatively. Survey respondents were most likely to believe that DPD officers are apt to stop people on the street or in their cars without good reason: 37 percent said they thought that police stopping people without justification was somewhat or very common in their neighborhoods (see Figure 2.2). About one-fifth of respondents believed that use of excessive force by DPD officers in their neighborhood was somewhat or very common. Similar percentages of respondents believed that use of offensive language by police officers was somewhat or very common (21 percent of the sample) or that police officers failing to abide by the law or police rules was somewhat or very common (23 percent of the sample).

Two items asked about fairness of the police (see Figure 2.3), again ranked on a four-point Likert scale. Respondents were overwhelmingly positive when asked about whether police officers in their neighborhoods treated citizens in a fair and courteous manner: 85 percent stated that the police were doing a good or very good job in this respect. Opinions about equal treatment of citizens by the police were less positive: 64 percent of respondents agreed or strongly agreed with the statement that DPD officers are generally unbiased in their dealings with citizens regardless of gender, ethnicity, religion, or sexual orientation. Conversely, one-fifth of persons surveyed strongly disagreed that the police dealt with all people in an unbiased manner.

The final set of questions about the police was concerned with police management and deployment (see Figure 2.4).[4] Respondents were evenly divided about whether there were

---

[2] See, for example, Miller and Davis, 2008.

[3] For the questions on police professionalism, we combined "don't know" responses with "never happens." This decision was based on experience from previous similar surveys in which a large percentage of respondents answered, "don't know" (in the present survey, this figure was 21 percent). This high nonresponse rate does not occur with other questions concerning opinions of the police. In several earlier surveys using the same items, respondents who answered "don't know" were questioned further about the reason for their answer. Overwhelmingly, they reported that they answered "don't know" because they had no knowledge that the police engaged in misconduct, which is virtually the same thing as saying that, as far as they are concerned, it never happens. Removing the "don't know" responses from the analysis reduces the "never happens" category by about 10 percentage points for the professionalism items.

[4] Each of these items was measured on a four-point Likert scale. For example, response options on the question about satisfaction with presence of police on the streets ranged from "very satisfied" to "somewhat satisfied" to "somewhat dissatisfied" to "very dissatisfied."

Figure 2.2
Opinions of Police Professionalism

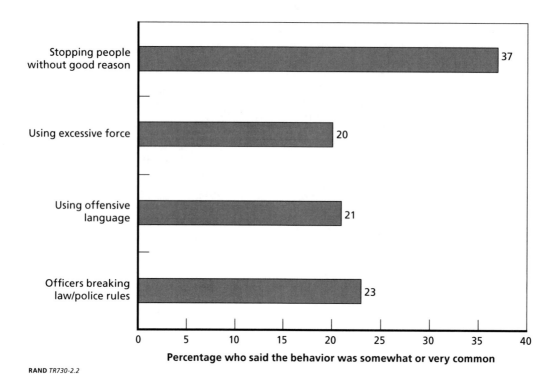

RAND *TR730-2.2*

Figure 2.3
Opinions of Police Fairness

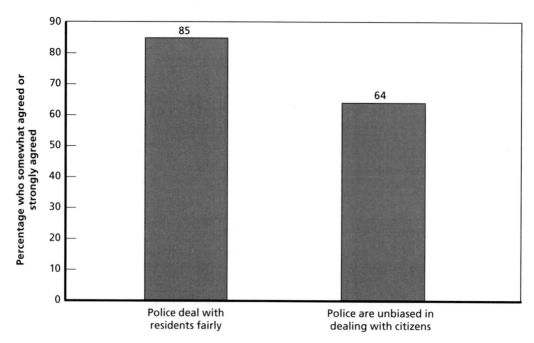

RAND *TR730-2.3*

Figure 2.4
Opinions of Police Management

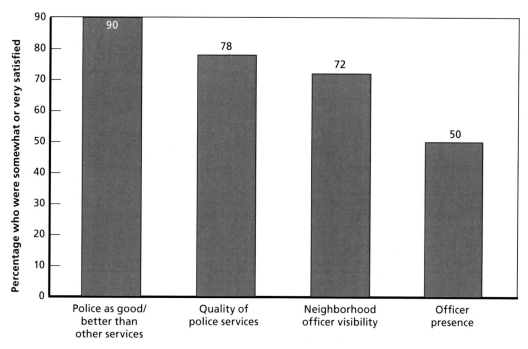

enough police officers on the street: Exactly half believed that the number of officers was sufficient, and half did not. A somewhat larger percentage expressed satisfaction with police presence in their neighborhood: 72 percent were very or somewhat satisfied with the presence of
police (in the form of uniformed officers seen in their neighborhoods), while 28 percent were
dissatisfied. (The discrepancy between this and the previous item may result from the word-
ing of the similar questions. The former question asked about DPD deployment in general,
while the latter asked about deployment in respondents' neighborhoods.) Other questions in
this section asked about satisfaction with police relative to other city services. Seventy-eight
percent of respondents were very or somewhat satisfied with the quality of police services, and
about the same proportion (74 percent) were satisfied with city services generally. When asked
to compare police services with other city services, a majority of respondents (51 percent) saw
no difference. But those who did see a difference were likely to favor the police: 30 percent of
such respondents believed that police services were superior to other city services, while just
10 percent believed that police services were worse.

Neighborhood Crime and Disorder Problems
Six survey items asked respondents about neighborhood problems, including car break-ins,
home break-ins, violent street crime, people selling or using drugs, fear of going out at night,
and youths loitering or committing vandalism. Response options were "very worried," "somewhat worried," and "not at all worried."

A majority of residents reported being very or somewhat worried about each of these
forms of disorder (see Figure 2.5). Of the indicators, the most commonly cited as a problem was worry about having one's home broken into (74 percent of respondents were very or

Figure 2.5
Perceptions of Neighborhood Problems

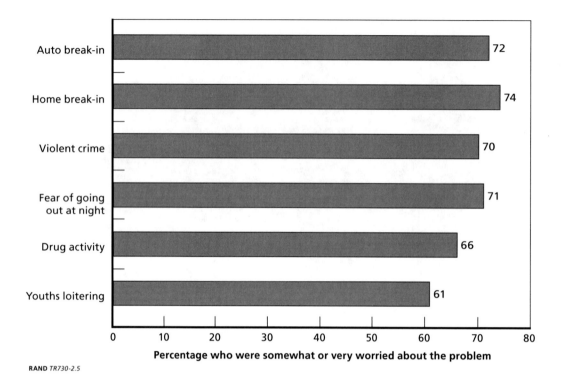

RAND *TR730-2.5*

somewhat worried), followed closely by having one's car broken into (72 percent were very or somewhat worried), being out in one's neighborhood at night (71 percent were very or somewhat worried), and being robbed or assaulted (70 percent were very or somewhat worried). Somewhat fewer residents were concerned about people selling or using drugs (66 percent were very or somewhat worried) and about youths loitering, panhandling, or committing vandalism (61 percent were very or somewhat worried).

The final set of items asked about actual victimization during the past year, specifically about having one's car or home broken into and being a victim of a violent street crime (see Figure 2.6). By far the most common crime reported was having one's car broken into: Auto larcenies were reported by 32 percent of respondents. Thirteen percent had their homes broken into. Roughly 1 in 10 respondents reported being the victim of an assault (10 percent) or robbery (9 percent) during the past year.[5]

---

[5]   The victimization rates reported here are very high. In contrast to the Department of Justice's National Crime Victimization Survey (NCVS), the questions about victimization in the Dallas survey were brief and straightforward. We expect that many people did not understand completely what is meant by "robbery" (people often confuse theft with robbery, for example) and by the other crimes they were asked about. Measuring victimization accurately, as the NCVS attempts to do, requires a 30–45 minute interview. That clearly was beyond the scope of what we were trying to do with the Dallas survey, which was focused on measuring public opinion of the police.

Figure 2.6
Victimization During Past Year

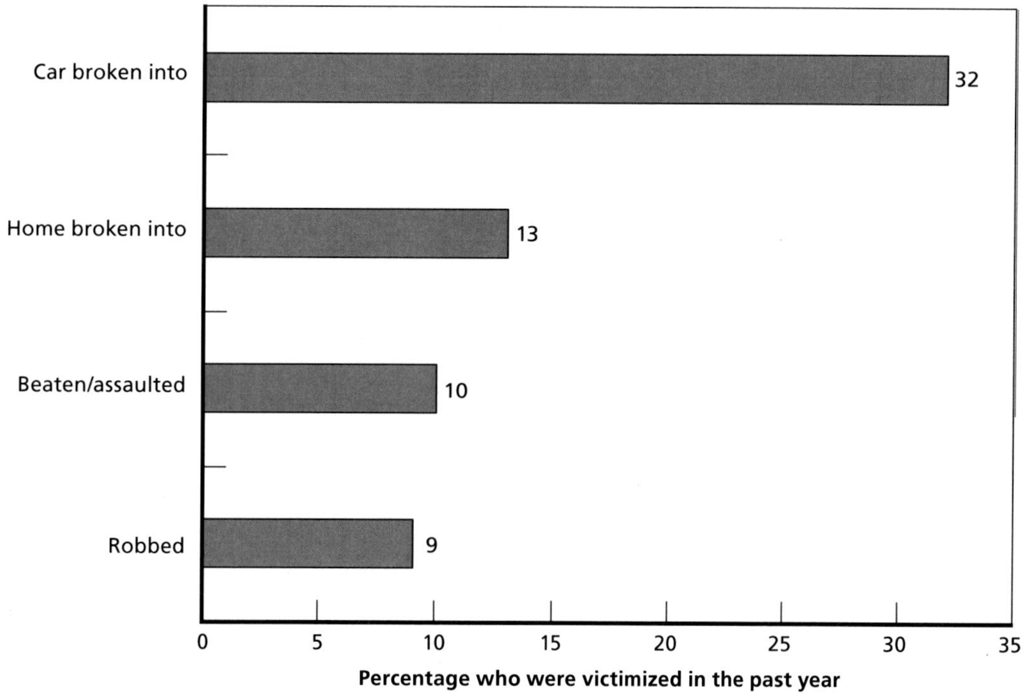

RAND TR730-2.6

Division Comparisons

This section breaks down survey results by Dallas's seven police divisions.[6] Opinions of the police are influenced by demographics as much as they are by police-citizen interactions (Miller and Davis, 2008). Since the demographic make-up of the divisions varies markedly, attempts to interpret comparisons must be undertaken cautiously. We present first comparisons between divisions using raw percentages on the individual items measuring police effectiveness, police conduct, and neighborhood problems. Then, for each of these domains, we create summary scales and test for statistical reliability of differences between divisions using statistical controls to adjust for the effects of age, race, and gender—three factors that previous research has found to influence opinions of the police.[7]

Opinions of the Police

Police Effectiveness. On the individual items of police effectiveness, the ratings were fairly consistent across divisions. Table 2.1 presents the proportion of respondents who rated their division police positively—that is, they rated them as very much or somewhat helpful to victims, as very or somewhat effective in fighting crime, etc. On the question about being help-

---

[6]   Unlike data reported in the previous section, the division comparisons are unweighted. This is because, in the analyses comparing divisions, we instead use statistical controls to neutralize effects of age, race, and gender.

[7]   See, for example, Skogan, 2005. We controlled for race, age, and gender in comparing divisions, since these are variables that are indicated as influencing opinions of the police in the literature. It is possible also that other, unmeasured, demographic variations may account for any observed differences between divisions in opinions of the police.

Table 2.1
Opinions of Police Effectiveness: Division Comparisons

Opinion	Percentage Who Somewhat or Strongly Agree, by Division							
	Central	North-east	South-east	South-west	North-west	North Central	South Central	Average
The police are effective in fighting crime.	84	88	78	87	85	92	75	84
The police respond promptly to calls.	62	64	52	58	57	59	52	58
The police are helpful to victims.	65	69	64	67	62	62	64	64
The police are good at working with residents.	76	76	62	72	78	77	66	72
The police are effective solving problems.	74	71	57	70	73	74	67	70

ful to victims, only seven percentage points differentiated the highest- from the lowest-rated division. Other items showed somewhat more variation: On the questions about working with residents to solve neighborhood problems and effectiveness at dealing with problems that concern neighborhood residents, the highest- and lowest-ranking divisions were separated by 16 and 17 percentage points, respectively.

No one division consistently led the others on measures of effectiveness. To determine whether there were consistent differences across divisions, we created a composite scale that effectively took the mean of the five items assessing police effectiveness.[8] The scale had good internal consistency, with a reliability coefficient of 0.89.[9] That is, the items are highly intercorrelated, indicating that they are measuring a single construct of police effectiveness. The scale ranged from 1 to 4, with scores of 3 or 4 indicating a positive evaluation.[10]

As mentioned earlier, different subpopulations typically have contrasting opinions of the police. Women tend to rate the police more highly than men; older people tend to rate the police more highly than younger people, and whites tend to rate the police more highly than blacks (Hispanics typically fall between blacks and whites).[11]

To reduce the effects of demographic differences between divisions, we conducted a test of statistical significance that held constant the effects of age, race, and gender. A summary of the test results are reported in Table 2.2, with the detailed results contained in Appendix B. The table shows that, as expected, opinions of the police were higher among women, older residents, and whites. However, even after accounting for these demographic factors, there remained a statistically significant effect of division. Closer inspection showed that police in Northeast and North Central divisions were perceived by residents as being more effective

---

[8]   Fourteen percent of the responses to the five survey items were answered "don't know." These items were simply omitted from the calculation, and the mean was based on the remaining valid responses.

[9]   Reliability coefficients range from 0 to 1. Values over 0.70 are considered acceptable.

[10]   Before creating the scale, the composite items were reversed-coded in order to make the scale more intuitive. A high score on the index indicates positive community opinion of effectiveness; a low score, negative community opinion.

[11]   See, for example, Reisig and Parks, 2000.

Table 2.2
Results of Multivariate Analysis of Division Differences in Police Effectiveness

Factor	Analysis Results
Age	Older residents believe that police are more effective than do younger residents.
Gender	Women believe that police are more effective than do men.
Race	Whites believe police that are more effective than do blacks or Hispanics.
Division	Residents of Northeast and North Central divisions believe that police are more effective, relative to the city average. Residents of Southeast and South Central divisions believe that police are less effective, relative to the city average.

than the citywide average, while police in Southeast and South Central divisions were believed to be less effective than the citywide average.

The ranking of the divisions is depicted in Figure 2.7. Divisions with scores significantly more positive than the citywide average are shown in green, those no different statistically from the city average in black, and those significantly lower than the city average in red (after controlling for effects of demographic factors).

Police Professionalism. Differences were sharper on some of the questions assessing police professionalism (see Table 2.3). For example, on the question asking about whether police stop citizens without good reason, a full 30 percentage points separated the highest- from the lowest-ranked division. For these items, the share of respondents indicating a problem was two to three times greater in the lowest-ranked division than in the highest-ranked division.

Figure 2.7
Opinions of Police Effectiveness: Division Comparisons

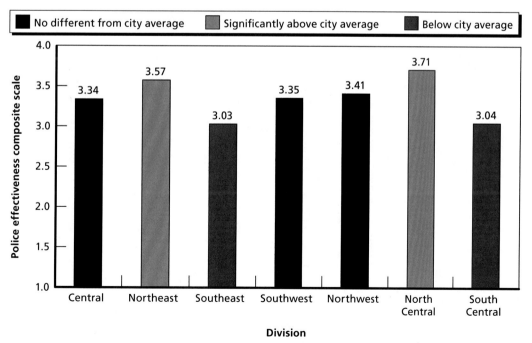

Table 2.3
Police Professionalism: Division Comparisons

Behavior	Percentage Who Say It Is Somewhat or Very Common, by Division							
	Central	North-east	South-east	South-west	North-west	North Central	South Central	Average
Police stop people without reason.	26	15	41	30	24	17	45	29
Police use excessive force.	11	10	25	15	11	11	24	15
Police use offensive language.	15	8	22	15	13	10	19	15
Police break law or rules.	16	10	30	18	10	12	20	17

The pattern of responses by division mirrored the pattern seen in the section on police effectiveness. Northeast and North Central divisions were the places where respondents were *least* likely to believe that the police were engaging in unprofessional behavior. On the other hand, Southeast and South Central divisions were the places where residents were most likely to perceive a problem with police professionalism. For example, only 15 percent and 17 percent respectively of residents in Northeast and North Central divisions believed that police officers stopping people on the street or in their cars was very or somewhat common: These figures contrast with 41 percent in Southeast division and 45 percent in South Central division who believed that DPD officers stopped people without reason.

As with the effectiveness items, we created a composite scale of police professionalism and calculated the mean values of the four items. The police professionalism scale had good internal consistency (reliability coefficient = 0.79), indicating that items are measuring a unitary construct. Values on the scale ranged from 1 to 5.

In order to attempt to mitigate the effects of demographic differences between divisions, we conducted a test of statistical significance that controlled for age, race, and gender. Table 2.4 summarizes the result of the analysis that is reported in full in Appendix B. In accordance with past research, we found that young people, males, blacks, and Hispanics were likely to have lower opinions of police professionalism than older residents, females, and whites. After accounting for these demographic factors, we still observed a statistically significant effect of police division. Further analysis of individual divisions revealed that only Southeast division differed significantly from the citywide average (it was lower) after the demographic factors were held constant.

Table 2.4
Results of Multivariate Analysis of Division Differences in Police Professionalism

Factor	Analysis Results
Age	Older residents believe police are more professional than do younger residents.
Gender	Women believe police are more professional than do men.
Race	Whites believe police are more professional than do blacks or Hispanics.
Division	Residents of Southeast division believe that police are less professional, relative to the city average.

Figure 2.8 ranks the divisions on the professionalism scale. Divisions with scores significantly more positive than the citywide average are shown in green, those no different statistically from the city average in black, and those significantly lower than the city average in red (after controlling for effects of demographic factors). The only district that differed significantly from the citywide average was the Southeast.

Neighborhood Crime and Disorder Problems

There was also a good deal of variation between the divisions on measures of perceived crime and disorder problems (see Table 2.5). On most of the six items, the proportion of respondents who were somewhat or very worried about crime and disorder problems ranged from

Figure 2.8
Opinions of Police Professionalism: Division Comparisons

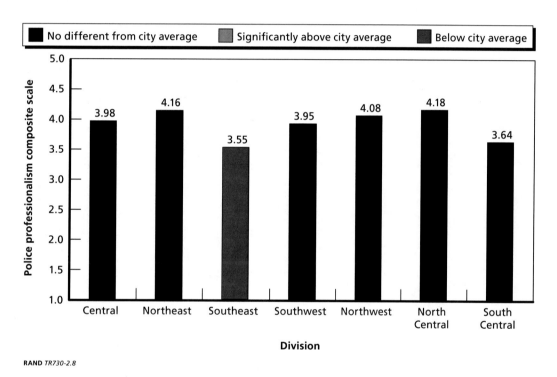

RAND TR730-2.8

Table 2.5
Perceptions of Neighborhood Problems: Division Comparisons

Concern	Percentage Who Are Somewhat or Very Worried, by Division							
	Central	North-east	South-east	South-west	North-west	North Central	South Central	Average
Auto larceny	78	62	71	62	75	57	67	67
Home break-in	71	72	80	69	81	67	70	72
Assault/robbery	74	66	66	64	68	63	72	68
Being out at night	79	68	71	70	68	62	75	71
Drug selling/use	60	59	73	69	63	43	76	64
Youths loitering	60	45	60	56	44	43	76	55

about 40 percent in some divisions to as much as 80 percent in others. The greatest variation between divisions was on the questions about drug selling/use and youth loitering, for which responses ranged from 43 percent in North Central division to 76 percent in South Central division. Over the six items, residents of Northeast division were least likely to express concerns. Residents of Central division were more concerned than other Dallas residents about auto larcenies, violent crime, and being out in the neighborhood at night, while residents of South Central division were more concerned than residents of other divisions about drug sales and use and youths loitering.

We combined the separate items into a neighborhood crime and disorder index by taking the mean value of the six items.[12] Internal consistency on the neighborhood disorder composite scale was on a par with the other two scales (reliability coefficient = 0.86). Scores on the index ranged from 1 to 3.

Table 2.6 presents a summary of the multivariate analysis of division differences on the neighborhood problem index, again holding constant the effects of age, gender, and race (see Appendix B for the details of the analysis). The analysis showed higher estimates of neighborhood problems among women and Hispanics relative to males and whites. After accounting for these demographic variables, North Central division residents reported fewer neighborhood problems than residents citywide, while residents of Central, Southeast, and South Central divisions each reported more neighborhood problems than the citywide average.

Figure 2.9 presents neighborhood problem scores by division. Divisions with scores significantly more positive than the citywide average are shown in green, those no different statistically from the city average in black, and those significantly lower than the city average in red (after controlling for effects of demographic factors).

Rates of actual victimizations reported by respondents showed remarkably little variation among divisions (see Table 2.7). The exceptions to this were home break-ins in South Central division (where 18 percent of respondents reported a burglary compared to the overall average of 11 percent); assaults and robberies in Northeast division (where just 2 percent of respondents reported being assaulted or robbed in the past year compared to an overall average of 5 percent); and assaults and robberies in Central division (where 9 percent of residents reported being assaulted or robbed compared to 5 percent citywide).

Table 2.6
Results of Multivariate Analysis of Division Differences in Neighborhood Problems

Factor	Analysis Results
Age	No difference between older and younger residents.
Gender	Women perceive more neighborhood problems than do men.
Race	Hispanics (but not blacks) perceive more neighborhood problems than do whites.
Division	Residents of North Central division perceive fewer neighborhood problems, relative to the city average. Residents of Central, Southeast, and South Central divisions perceive more neighborhood problems, relative to the city average.

---

[12] The 5 percent of the responses to the five survey items answered "don't know" were omitted from the calculation, and the mean was based on the remaining valid responses.

Figure 2.9
Perceptions of Neighborhood Problems: Division Comparisons

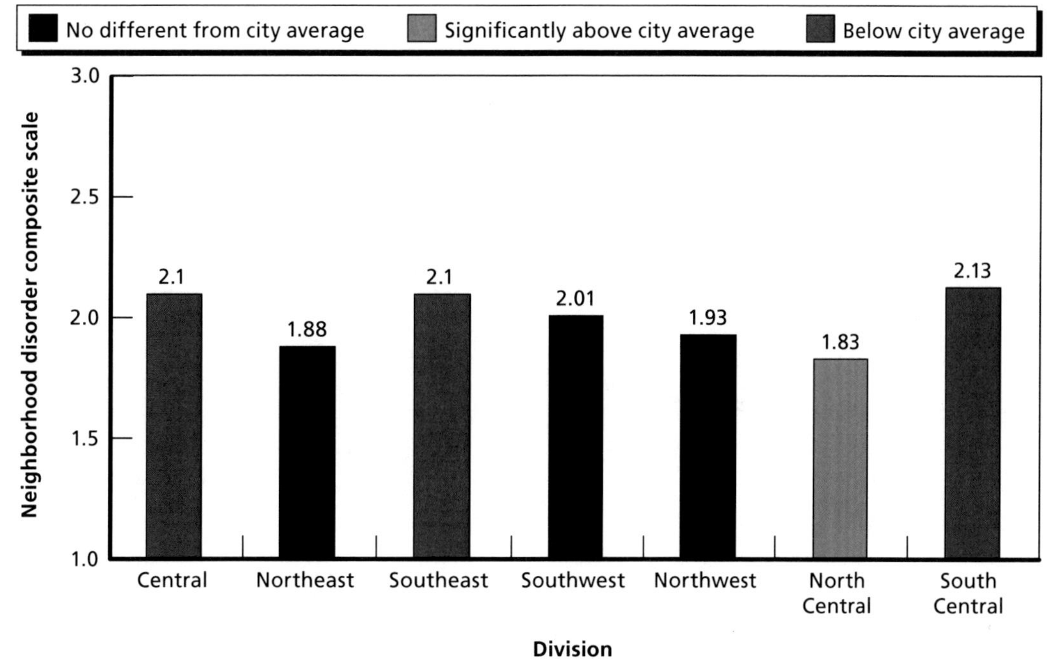

RAND TR730-2.9

Table 2.7
Victimization in Past 12 Months: Division Comparisons

Crime	Percentage Who Have Been a Victim in the Past 12 Months, by Division							
	Central	North-east	South-east	South-west	North-west	North Central	South Central	Average
Car break-in/theft	25	19	28	21	23	18	27	23
Home break-in	11	9	14	12	9	3	18	11
Beating/assault	9	2	6	3	5	4	7	5
Robbery	9	2	5	5	5	3	6	5

Comparison of Dallas with Other Municipalities

In this section, we provide comparisons of opinions of the police between Dallas and other municipalities. We present two sets of comparisons. The first set contrasts Dallas to other major cities in which we have used the same survey items. The comparison cities include New York, Chicago, Washington, D.C., Pittsburgh, and Seattle. In these cities, the same survey questions were used as we have used in Dallas on police effectiveness and police professionalism. However, the surveys were done at different times and by different survey companies, so the results are not strictly comparable. There may have been differences in the methodologies used by the different survey companies or differences in the procedures used to weight the sample data to population parameters. Moreover, there have been national shifts in opinions of the police over time as a result of the 9/11 attacks and other factors.

With those caveats in mind, Tables 2.8 and 2.9 compare the survey results in Dallas with the other cities. Table 2.8 shows that the DPD was rated substantially higher on measures of police effectiveness relative to the other cities. The differences were apparent across all of the effectiveness items, but most pronounced in the question about being helpful to crime victims. While 81 percent of Dallas residents thought that the police were helpful or very helpful toward crime victims, in Seattle—the next highest ranked city—only 57 percent of residents felt that way.

Table 2.9 compares Dallas with the other major metropolitan areas on measures of police professionalism. Here, we have just two comparable questions. On the first—stopping people without good reason—the DPD fell roughly in the middle of the group. On the other—use of offensive language—Dallas residents rated the police as substantially better than residents of Seattle, New York, or Pittsburgh.

The DPD is taking part in an effort by RAND and the Commission on Accreditation for Law Enforcement Agencies to develop and test performance metrics that will enable comparison of police agencies on a range of different dimensions. In Dallas; Knoxville, Tennessee; Broward County, Florida; and Kettering, Ohio, identical surveys have been conducted examining community opinion of the police: While the sites were picked for their dissimilarity (they

Table 2.8
Opinions of Police Effectiveness in Dallas and Other Major Cities

Opinion	Percentage Who Somewhat or Strongly Agree, by City					
	Dallas 2008	New York 1997	Washington, D.C., 1999	Chicago 2003	Seattle 2003	Pittsburgh 2004
The police do a good job preventing crime.	81	50	53	60	73	63
The police promptly respond to nonemergency calls.	65	NA	NA	51	56	NA
The police are helpful to crime victims.	81	38	36	NA	57	67
The police are effective in dealing with problems that concern people.	77	48	57	NA	63	59
The police work together with residents to solve local problems.	79	35	49	54	52	53

NOTE: NA = not asked.

Table 2.9
Opinions of Police Professionalism in Dallas and Other Major Cities

Behavior	Percentage Who Perceieve It as a Minor or Major Problem					
	Dallas 2008	New York 1997	Washington, D.C., 1999	Chicago 2003	Seattle 2003	Pittsburgh 2004
Police stopping people without good reason	37	45	20	33	50	63
Police using offensive language	21	53	NA	NA	27	51

NOTE: NA = not asked.

included a small Southern city, a Midwestern town, and an urban Southern county), these surveys were all carried out by the Schaeffer Center at about the same time using the same questionnaires. We include the data from these sites for the sake of interest, not because these municipalities constitute a fair standard against which to measure Dallas.

Figure 2.10 shows the results from the four sites for the police effectiveness scale. Kettering was rated the highest of the four by respondents. Dallas was similar to the other two sites.

Figure 2.11 compares the four locales on the police professionalism scale. Again, Kettering was ranked highest, and Dallas was comparable to the other two law enforcement agencies.

Conclusion

The community survey suggests that most Dallas residents have a good deal of confidence in their police department. Some of the areas where there is room for improvement include perceptions of response time, unjustified stops, and equal treatment of residents regardless of gender, ethnicity, religion, and sexual orientation. Methodologically, we learned that standard sampling methods may not be sufficient to obtain proportional representation of Hispanic households in the survey. Future surveys will explore ways to increase the proportion of Hispanic respondents without the need to draw a separate Hispanic sample.

Figure 2.10
Opinions of Police Effectiveness: Comparison of Dallas with Other Municipalities

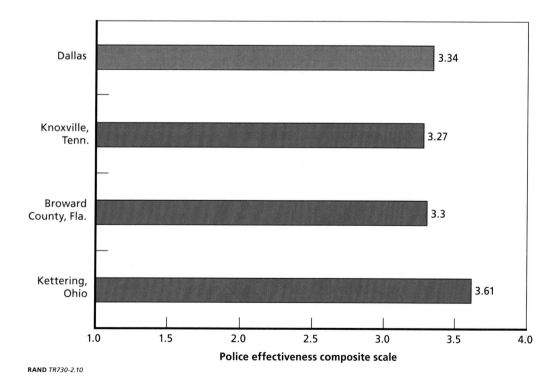

RAND *TR730-2.10*

Figure 2.11
Opinions of Police Professionalism: Comparison of Dallas with Other Municipalities

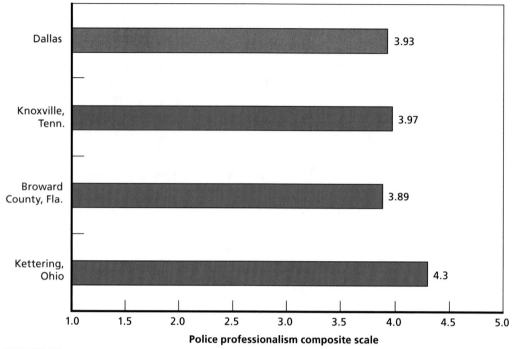

RAND *TR730-2.11*

CHAPTER THREE

Satisfaction with Police Encounters

Highlights

- Between 70 and 90 percent of Dallas residents who had recently called the police to report a victimization were satisfied or very satisfied with how the responding officers handled the incident. Respondents were most satisfied with how respectfully they were treated by the officer(s) and less satisfied with how quickly police responded to the incident.
- Dallas residents who had a recent involuntary contact with the police (i.e., received a summons) were somewhat less satisfied with the interaction than residents who had a recent voluntary contact with the police. Still, approximately two-thirds of involuntary contact respondents or more were somewhat or very satisfied with all aspects of the encounter.
- There were no significant differences between divisions in satisfaction with voluntary police contacts. Residents of one division (South Central) were less satisfied with involuntary contacts than residents of the other divisions.
- Satisfaction rates for Dallas residents who had either a voluntary or involuntary contact with the police were similar to rates for other agencies where similar surveys have been conducted.

Introduction

This section of the interim report summarizes the results of telephone surveys with persons who had had recent contact with officers of the DPD. Respondents included roughly equal numbers of persons who had a recent voluntary contact with law enforcement (reported a property crime) or a recent involuntary contact (issued a traffic or class C summons). The 577 voluntary contact surveys and 532 involuntary contact surveys were roughly evenly divided according to which of the city's seven police divisions that the encounter occurred. Surveys were conducted by the Survey Center at George Mason University from lists supplied by the DPD of persons who had a recent law enforcement encounter.[1] Surveys were completed with 81 percent of persons contacted who had had a voluntary encounter with the police and with 74 percent of persons contacted who had had received a traffic or quality-of-life summons.

The brief surveys drew their content from surveys developed and tested at the Vera Institute of Justice in cooperation with the New York City Police Department in 2001–2002. The

---

[1] Potential respondents were drawn from persons who had had a contact with a DPD officer during the past three months.

Vera surveys were administered monthly to 5,000 people who had recent contact with the police because they reported a crime or had been issued a summons (Vera Institute of Justice and the Lieberman Research Group, 2003). Unlike community opinion surveys, the Vera work indicated that responses to the questions were not greatly influenced by age, race, or gender. This suggests that people were able to isolate their perception of how the specific incident was handled from preexisting attitudes toward the police.[2]

Both the voluntary contact and involuntary contact surveys include seven questions on satisfaction with the way the police officer or officers handled the encounter. Each question included response options on a four-point Likert scale (e.g., the officer treated me very professionally, somewhat professionally, somewhat unprofessionally, very unprofessionally). Questions on the voluntary contact survey included the following:

- How professionally would you say that the officer(s) treated you?
- How respectfully were you treated by the officers?
- How well did the officer(s) explain where you could get help for problems you might have had as a result of the incident?
- How knowledgeable were the officers in dealing with the problems you were experiencing?
- How interested was the officer(s) in your problem?
- How promptly did the police respond to your situation?
- Overall, how satisfied were you with how the officer(s) handled your situation?

Questions on the involuntary contact survey were similar, and included the following:

- How professionally would you say that the officer(s) treated you?
- How respectfully were you treated by the officers?
- How clear was the officer(s) in explaining why you were stopped?
- Was any force used by the officer(s) to detain you appropriate?
- Did the officer(s) explain whether you needed to do anything after the encounter was over?
- Would you say that the time that you were detained was reasonable?
- Overall, how satisfied were you with how the officer(s) handled your situation?

We first summarize the citywide and division results of each item on the two surveys. Then we integrate the survey items into a two summary measures and compare the divisions on the composite measures. Finally, we compare the contact survey results for Dallas with results obtained using the same surveys in other jurisdictions.

Citywide Results

Figure 3.1 displays responses to the voluntary contact survey items. Percentages in the table represent the percentage of respondents who answered "strongly agree" or "somewhat agree"

---

[2]   While other work tends to support the idea that demographics play a minimal role in determining satisfaction with police encounters, some differences have been found between blacks and other ethnic groups in satisfaction with involuntary encounters; see Skogan, 2005, and Bureau of Justice Statistics, 2002.

Figure 3.1
Summary Responses to Voluntary Contact Survey Questions

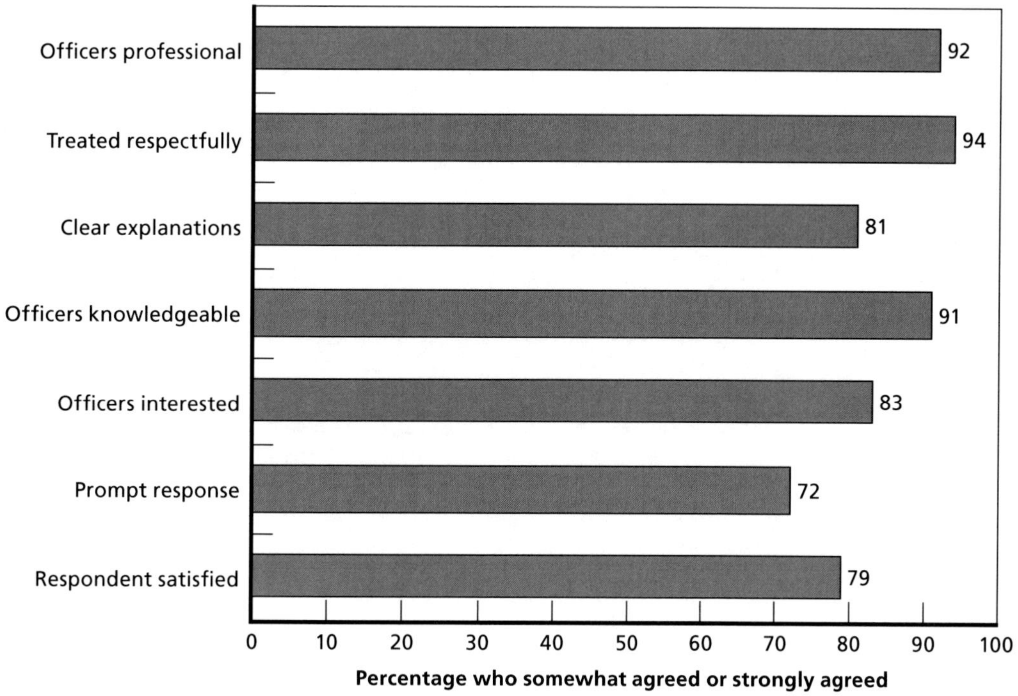

Question	Percentage who somewhat agreed or strongly agreed
Officers professional	92
Treated respectfully	94
Clear explanations	81
Officers knowledgeable	91
Officers interested	83
Prompt response	72
Respondent satisfied	79

Percentage who somewhat agreed or strongly agreed

RAND TR730-3.1

to each of the items. Overall, the responses were very positive. Officers received the highest marks—more than 90 percent favorable ratings—for treating citizens respectfully and for being knowledgeable about how to deal with respondents' problems. Officers were rated somewhat lower for the promptness of the response (roughly 70 percent positive ratings), giving clear explanations of where respondents could get help for problems arising from their victimization, and showing interest in respondents' situations (each with about 80 percent in favorable ratings).

Figure 3.2 summarizes responses to the involuntary contact questionnaire items. Not surprisingly, persons subject to an involuntary contact with DPD officers were less positive about their encounter than persons who contacted the police for assistance. Still, a majority of involuntary contact respondents were favorable in their evaluation of police officers who detained them. In 81 percent of the cases, respondents indicated that no force was used, but, among the 19 percent of cases in which force was used, nearly half of the respondents believed that the police used inappropriate force in the stop. More than 75 percent of respondents thought that the officers acted professionally and respectfully and that they gave a reasonable explanation for the stop.

Slightly lower percentages of respondents believed that the officers explained any additional obligations that they needed to satisfy and that the time they were detained was reasonable. About two-thirds of respondents reported that they were satisfied with the overall way in which the officers handled their situations.

Figure 3.2
Summary Responses to Involuntary Contact Survey Questions

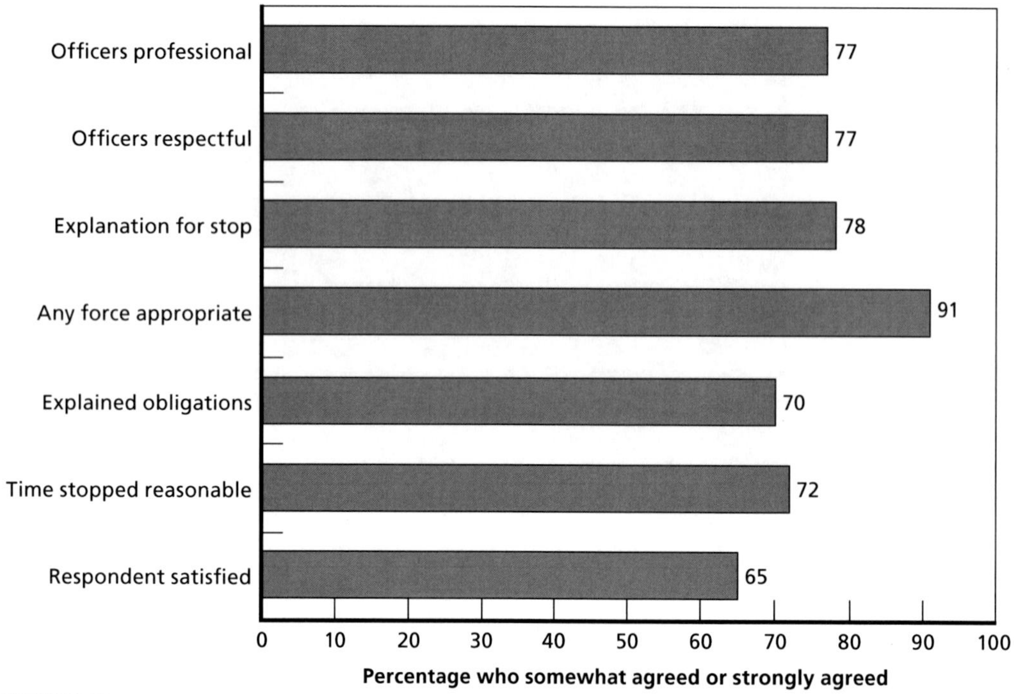

RAND *TR730-3.2*

Comparison of Results by Division

Next, we break down the results of the two surveys by police division. Table 3.1 summarizes the results of respondents who had a voluntary contact with a law enforcement officer in each of the seven police divisions. The percentages in the table represent the proportion of respondents who gave a positive evaluation to each of the seven items (those who were very or somewhat satisfied with the way the situation was handled, etc.). The table shows a high degree of consistency across divisions. In most cases, the difference between the highest- and lowest-ranked division was 10 percentage points or less. The largest difference was on the question about response time, where 19 percentage points differentiated the Southwest division (77 percent positive ratings) from the South Central division (58 percent positive ratings).

Table 3.2 presents positive responses to the questions for involuntary contact respondents by division. Variations between divisions here tended to be somewhat larger, with 10 percentage points or greater differences on most of the items. The largest difference was 19 percentage points, which separated the North Central division (86 percent positive rating) from the South Central division (67 percent positive rating) on officer professionalism; 19 percentage points also separated the North Central division (79 percent positive ratings) from the South Central division (60 percent positive ratings) on reasonableness of time detained.

To determine whether there were consistent differences across divisions, we created a composite scale that effectively took the mean of the seven items assessing satisfaction with voluntary and involuntary police contacts. The two scales had good internal consistency (alpha coefficient = 0.88 for each). That is, the items that comprise each scale are highly inter-correlated,

Table 3.1
Satisfaction with Voluntary Contacts: Division Comparisons

Percentage of Respondents Who	Division							
	Central	North-east	South-east	South-west	North-west	North Central	South Central	Average
Believed officers acted professionally	93	89	88	94	90	94	94	92
Believed officers treated them respectfully	95	93	95	93	93	98	94	94
Believed officers explained clearly where to get help	85	79	86	79	78	82	77	81
Believed officers were knowledgeable in dealing with their problem	90	93	96	88	90	87	90	91
Believed that officers were interested in helping	76	83	90	93	79	77	84	83
Believed that officers responded promptly	72	70	75	77	67	77	58	72
Were satisfied with the way in which their situation was handled	76	78	79	86	75	81	78	79

Table 3.2
Satisfaction with Involuntary Contacts: Division Comparisons

Percentage of Respondents Who	Division							
	Central	North-east	South-east	South-west	North-west	North Central	South Central	Average
Believed officers acted professionally	73	82	69	81	80	86	67	77
Believed officers treated them respectfully	73	85	73	77	81	80	66	77
Believed officers explained clearly reason for stop	78	77	80	81	86	78	69	78
Believed officers used force appropriate to situation	96	98	97	96	99	95	91	96
Believed that officers explained any additional obligations	71	76	62	73	73	72	63	70
Believed that time detained was reasonable	72	72	75	76	78	79	60	72
Were satisfied with the way in which their situation was handled	64	67	71	66	71	68	52	65

indicating that they are measuring a single construct of satisfaction with the encounter. The scales ranged from 1 to 4, with scores of 3 or 4 indicating a positive evaluation.[3]

Figure 3.3 compares divisions on satisfaction with voluntary contacts with the police. There was little difference between divisions: Scores were bunched between 3.3 and 3.45, or between a positive and very positive evaluation of the encounter. The slight differences between districts did not approach statistical significance.[4]

Figure 3.4 displays division scores on the involuntary contact satisfaction summary measure. Again, there were only minor differences between most of the divisions, ranging from 3.29 to 3.16. However, South Central division was rated substantially lower than the others, with a mean satisfaction score of 2.89. An overall test of statistical significance confirmed that there was a reliable difference between the divisions.[5] Planned contrasts indicated that the South Central division average was significantly lower than the overall mean. (None of the other division averages differed significantly from the overall mean.)

Figure 3.3
Division Comparisons in Voluntary Contact Satisfaction Scale

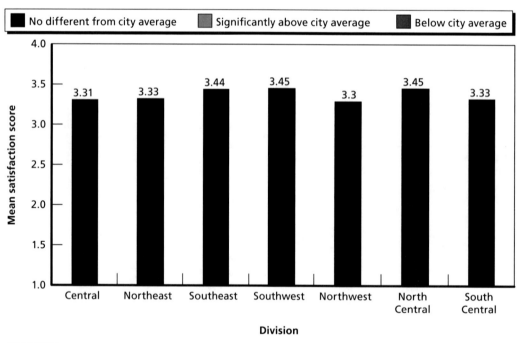

---

[3]   Before creating the scale, the composite items were reversed-coded in order to make the scale more intuitive. A high score on the index indicates positive evaluation of the interaction; a low score, negative evaluation.

[4] $F[6,570] = 0.81$, $p = 0.57$.

[5] $F[6,525] = 2.60$, $p = 0.02$.

Figure 3.4
Division Comparisons in Involuntary Contact Satisfaction Scale

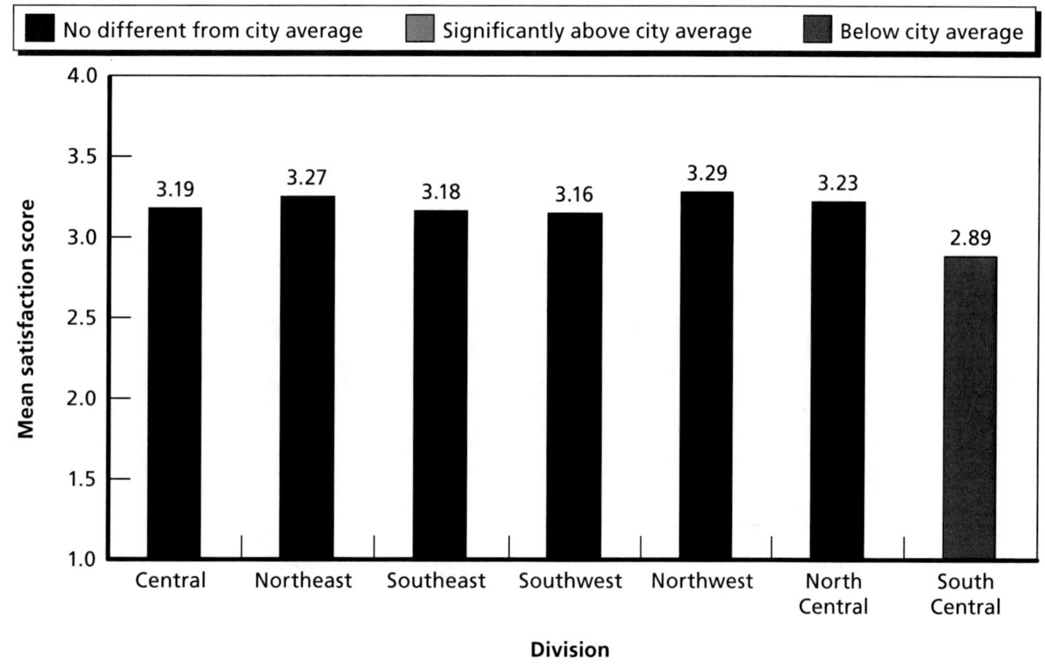

RAND TR730-3.4

How Dallas Compares with Some Other Jurisdictions

We have used the same surveys to measure satisfaction with police contacts in other jurisdictions. Figure 3.5 shows how Dallas compares with the other places where the surveys have been used. Ratings for voluntary contacts shown in Figure 3.5 were very similar across five law enforcement agencies. Dallas's rating of 3.37 was in the middle of the constricted range.

There was broader range in the distribution of involuntary contact scores across four sites, as shown in Figure 3.6. (The fifth site—New York City—is not included because the scale used was different than for the other sites.) The larger range may be, in part, due to different sampling frames in the different agencies: Some agencies provided lists that included only persons issued traffic citations, others provided lists that included summonses issued for nontraffic violations as well, and one agency provided a list of misdemeanor arrestees. Again, Dallas's rating was in the middle of the range.

Conclusion

In a real sense, people who call on the police for help and people who are detained by the police are significant "consumers" of policing services. The survey results indicate that both of these consumer groups were satisfied with the way that the interaction was handled by DPD officers. The fact that differences between divisions was minimal suggests that training and policy standards set by the central command are effected uniformly across the DPD.

Figure 3.5
Satisfaction with Voluntary Contacts: Comparison of Dallas with Other Municipalities

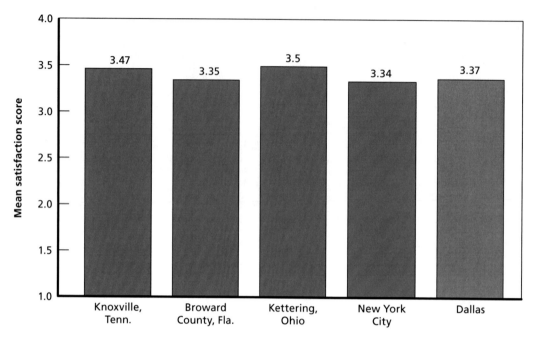

RAND *TR730-3.5*

Figure 3.6
Satisfaction with Involuntary Contacts: Comparison of Dallas with Other Municipalities

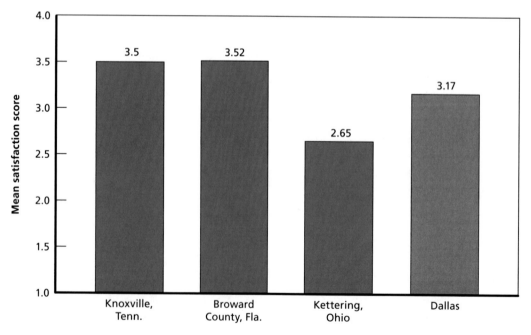

RAND *TR730-3.6*

CHAPTER FOUR

Surveys of Police Officers: Job Satisfaction, Opinions of Leadership, and Climate of Integrity

Highlights

- On items relating to job satisfaction, Dallas police officers were most likely to agree that they know what is expected of them on the job (87 percent agreement), that their supervisor cares about them (65 percent agreement), and that their co-workers are committed to doing quality work. Officers were least likely to agree that they receive praise for doing good work (30 percent agreement), that their opinions at work count (40 percent agreement), and that someone at work encourages their development (41 percent agreement).
- Overall job satisfaction among DPD officers was somewhere between "somewhat satisfied" and "somewhat dissatisfied"—lower than the other three law enforcement agencies taking part in the performance indicators project. However, Dallas is the only major city agency among the four.
- On items relating to perceptions of leadership in the DPD, 83 percent of DPD officers felt that their immediate supervisor was available to them. However, perceptions of departmental leadership were not positive: Just one-third or fewer officers believed that departmental leaders communicate to officers what is expected of them (36 percent), are consistent in their expectations (14 percent), articulate a compelling vision of the work of the DPD (25 percent), motivate officers to perform exceptionally (13 percent), or hold themselves to high standards (23 percent).
- Dallas officers consistently rated hypothetical ethics infractions as more serious than the average from a national study, suggesting that the DPD has a better than average climate of integrity.

Introduction

This section presents the results of officer surveys that were conducted in Dallas in the spring of 2009. The surveys had three parts: job satisfaction items from the widely used Gallup Q12 survey (Thackery, 2001), perceptions of leadership based in part on the Multifactor Leadership Questionnaire (Avolio and Bass, 2008), and questions about the culture of integrity drawn from the work of Carl Klockars et al. (2000). The surveys were administered as Web-based questionnaires. Officers completed the surveys anonymously. The survey was completed by 668 (21 percent) of the 3,131 sworn staff of the DPD.

Job Satisfaction

The Gallup Q12 is a survey designed to measure employee engagement. The instrument was the result of hundreds of focus groups and interviews. Researchers found that there were 12 key expectations that, when satisfied, form the foundation of strong feelings of engagement. Tens of thousands of work units and more than 1 million employees have participated in the Q12 instrument. The instrument contains these 12 items, each ranked on a scale of 1 to 5 (strongly disagree to strongly agree):

- I know what is expected of me at work.
- I have the materials and equipment I need to do my work right.
- At work, I have the opportunity to do what I do best every day.
- In the last seven days, I have received recognition or praise for doing good work.
- My supervisor, or someone at work, seems to care about me as a person.
- There is someone at work who encourages my development.
- At work, my opinions seem to count.
- The mission/purpose of my company makes me feel my job is important.
- My associates (fellow employees) are committed to doing quality work.
- I have a best friend at work.
- In the last six months, someone at work has talked to me about my progress.
- This last year, I have had opportunities at work to learn and grow.

Survey results are summarized in Figure 4.1, which depicts the proportion of officers who agreed or strongly agreed with each of the 12 items. There was a large difference in the percentage of positive responses from item to item. Nearly 90 percent of officers who completed the survey said that expectations for their performance were clearly defined. About two-thirds of respondents believed that their supervisor cares about them as a person and that their fellow officers are committed to quality. On the other hand, less than half of officers who completed the survey felt that their opinions count, that their development is encouraged, or that someone at work had talked to them about their progress. An even smaller proportion of officers (about one-third) said that they had received praise for their work in the past week. Overall, some of the highest scores were on items having to do with relationships at work; some of the lowest had to do with acknowledgement and recognition.

Combining responses from the 12 items, we created a summary scale of job satisfaction.[1] Figure 4.2 compares job satisfaction in Dallas to officer satisfaction in three other law enforcement agencies. Dallas's rating of 3.28 indicates that the average response to the 12 items was slightly better than the neutral response, "neither agree nor disagree." Officer satisfaction in Dallas was lower than in the average in the other three agencies and, in fact, nearly a full point lower than the highest of the averages. The differences among agencies were statistically significant.[2]

---

[1]   The reliability coefficient for the 12 items is 0.88.

[2] $F[3,976] = 14.55$, $p < 0.001$.

Figure 4.1
Officers' Job Satisfaction

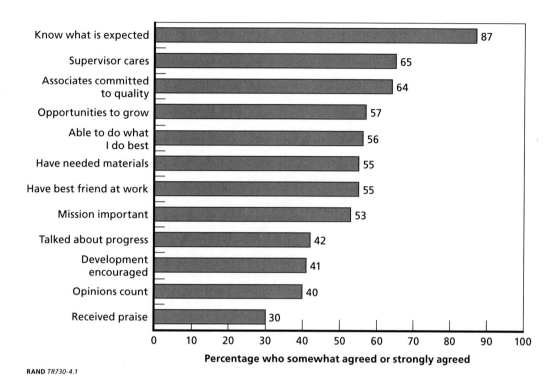

RAND *TR730-4.1*

Figure 4.2
Job Satisfaction in DPD and Other Law Enforcement Agencies

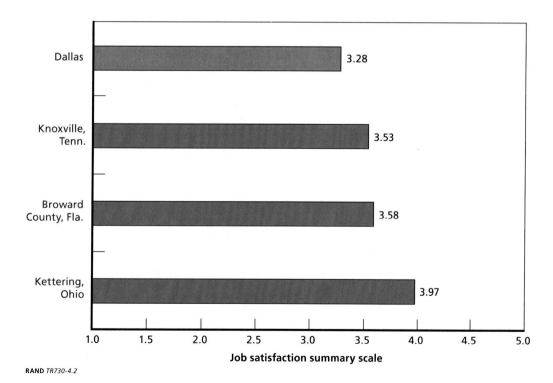

RAND *TR730-4.2*

Officers' Perceptions of Leadership

The leadership section of the Dallas officer survey drew questions from the Multi-Factor Leadership Questionnaire, supplemented with items from Police Foundation surveys utilized in operational studies of various police departments including Detroit, Washington, D.C., and Phoenix.

Figure 4.3 depicts the proportion of officers who agreed or strongly agreed with each of the leadership items. The most striking thing about the figure is there is a large discrepancy between officers' perceptions about leadership of their immediate supervisors and perceptions of departmental leaders. Just one-third or fewer officers believed that departmental leaders communicate to officers what is expected of them (36 percent), are consistent in their expectations (14 percent), articulate a compelling vision of the work of the DPD (25 percent), motivate officers to perform exceptionally (13 percent), or hold themselves to high standards (23 percent). On the other hand, majorities of officers believed that their direct supervisor is available to them (83 percent), provides useful information and guidance (62 percent), seeks differing perspectives in solving problems (62 percent), recognizes exceptional work (60 percent), provides inspiration for officers to perform at their best (53 percent), and motivates officers under their supervision (51 percent). Just over one-third of the officers believed that their supervisor spends time teaching and coaching (35 percent) or helps to develop officers' strengths (35 percent).

Figure 4.3
Officers' Opinions About Department Leadership

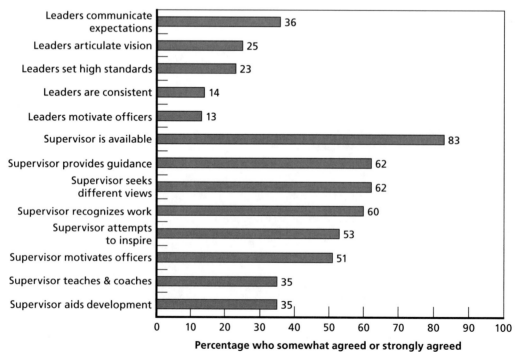

RAND *TR730-4.3*

Integrity

The integrity questionnaire developed by Klockars et al. (2000) was designed to elicit information on the culture of integrity of law enforcement agencies. The original version asked officers to rate each item in terms of seriousness, severity of discipline that the offense would or should incur, and willingness to report the incident. Respondents were asked to provide ratings from their own perspectives, from the perspectives of their co-workers, and the perspectives of their supervisors. We used an abbreviated version of the questionnaire, asking officers to rate only seriousness of the incident from their perspective and the perspective of their supervisors (see the "Case Scenarios" text box on the next page). Ratings were done according to a five-point scale ranging from "Not at all serious" to "Very serious."

The results of officers' ratings of seriousness are presented in Figure 4.4, in descending order of seriousness. Stealing a watch from the scene of a jewelry store burglary, failing to report a found wallet, accepting a bribe from a speeder, receiving a kickback from a body shop owner for making referrals, accepting free drinks in exchange for allowing a bar to remain open after hours, and supervisors giving time off in exchange for personal favors were almost universally considered serious infractions. Scenarios perceived as least serious were running a business installing security items on the side, accepting free meals or cigarettes from merchants, and failing to report an obviously intoxicated officer who drove his car into a ditch.

In Table 4.1, we compare the responses of Dallas officers with the responses of officers in three other law enforcement agencies and with Klockars et al.'s average of 29 law enforcement

Figure 4.4
Officer Ratings of Seriousness of Integrity Scenarios

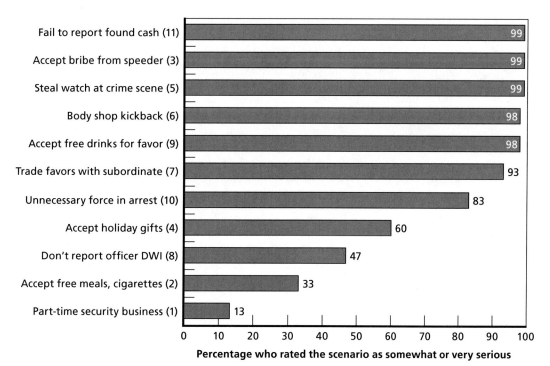

NOTE: The numbers in parentheses indicate the number of the scenario in the text box on the next page.

RAND *TR730-4.4*

Integrity Scenarios

Scenario 1. A police officer runs his own private business in which he sells and installs security devices, such as alarms, special locks, etc. He does this work during his off-duty hours.

Scenario 2. A police officer routinely accepts free meals, cigarettes, and other items of small value from merchants on his beat. He does not solicit these gifts and is careful not to abuse the generosity of those who give gifts to him.

Scenario 3. A police officer stops a motorist for speeding. The officer agrees to accept a personal gift of half of the amount of the fine in exchange for not issuing a citation.

Scenario 4. A police officer is widely liked in the community, and on holidays local merchants and restaurant and bar owners show their appreciation for his attention by giving him gifts of food and liquor.

Scenario 5. A police officer discovers a burglary of a jewelry shop. The display cases are smashed, and it is obvious that many items have been taken. While searching the shop, he takes a watch, worth about two days' pay for that officer. He reports that the watch had been stolen during the burglary.

Scenario 6. A police officer has a private arrangement with a local auto body shop to refer the owners of cars damaged in accidents to the shop. In exchange for each referral, he receives payment of 5 percent of the repair bill from the shop owner.

Scenario 7. A police officer, who happens to be a very good auto mechanic, is scheduled to work during coming holidays. A supervisor offers to give him these days off, if he agrees to tune up his supervisor's personal car. Evaluate the supervisor's behavior.

Scenario 8. At 2:00 a.m., a police officer, who is on duty, is driving his patrol car on a deserted road. He sees a vehicle that has been driven off the road and is stuck in a ditch. He approaches the vehicle and observes that the driver is not hurt but is obviously intoxicated. He also finds that the driver is a police officer. Instead of reporting this accident and offense, he transports the driver to his home.

Scenario 9. A police officer finds a bar on his beat that is still serving drinks a half-hour past its legal closing time. Instead of reporting this violation, the police officer agrees to accept a couple of free drinks from the owner.

Scenario 10. Two police officers on foot patrol surprise a man who is attempting to break into an automobile. The man flees. They chase him for about two blocks before apprehending him by tackling him and wrestling him to the ground. After he is under control, both officers punch him a couple of times in the stomach as punishment for fleeing and resisting.

Scenario 11. A police officer finds a wallet in a parking lot. It contains an amount of money equivalent to a full day's pay for that officer. He reports the wallet as lost property but keeps the money for himself.

Table 4.1
Officer Ratings of Seriousness of Scenario-Based Infractions

Mean Seriousness Rating	Dallas	Broward County, Fla.	Knoxville, Tenn.	Kettering, Ohio	29-City Average
Scenario 1: Part-time security business	1.93	1.95	2.07	1.35	1.46
Scenario 2: Accept free meals, cigarettes	2.81	3.54	2.94	3.00	2.60
Scenario 3: Accept bribe from speeder	4.97	4.98	4.95	4.95	4.92
Scenario 4: Accept holiday gifts	3.54	3.82	3.88	3.55	2.84
Scenario 5: Steal watch at crime scene	4.97	4.99	5.00	5.00	4.95
Scenario 6: Body shop kickback	4.82	4.86	4.79	4.90	4.50
Scenario 7: Trade favors with subordinate	4.55	4.54	4.44	4.50	4.18
Scenario 8: Don't report officer DWI	3.23	3.33	3.22	3.10	3.03
Scenario 9: Accept free drinks for favor	3.62	4.81	4.86	4.75	4.54
Scenario 10: Unnecessary force in arrest	4.23	4.46	4.50	4.15	4.05
Scenario 11: Fail to report found cash	4.92	4.95	4.96	4.95	4.85
11-item average seriousness rating	4.07	4.20	4.14	4.02	3.81

agencies. The results show a high degree of consistency across agencies for the most serious infractions—accepting bribes, stealing from a crime scene, and failing to report found cash. On the lesser infractions, however, responses among agencies differ substantially. On the scenario about accepting holiday gifts, for example, 0.7 points separated Dallas from Klockars et al.'s 29-city average. On the great majority of items, Dallas officers rated the infractions as more serious than the average agency in Klockars et al.'s study. Overall differences among the four agencies participating in the officer surveys were not large, but they were statistically significant.[3]

Conclusion

The results of the officer survey were mixed. Indications are that Dallas officers take ethics infractions more seriously than officers in many other departments. However, responses to various aspects of job satisfaction were mixed and, overall, less positive than responses to the same items from officers in other municipalities. Officers had generally positive opinions of their immediate supervisors, but not of the departmental leadership. We do not have comparison data from other municipalities on perceptions of leadership, but will have similar data for at least eight other agencies the next time this survey is conducted.

[3] $F[3,979] = 5.46, p < 0.001.$

CHAPTER FIVE

Satisfaction of Retail Business Owners with Policing

Highlights

- More than 70 percent of respondents in a small sample of Dallas retail business owners gave the DPD a positive rating for crime-fighting effectiveness and working with local businesses. For most other items (prompt response to calls, preventing crimes, maintaining a visible presence, and dealing with problems that concern businesses), the proportion of positive responses fell between 40 and 60 percent.

Introduction

In addition to the general public, there are specific interest groups who are consumers of police services. One of the most important of these is the commercial sector. With the help of the Dallas regional Chamber of Commerce, we surveyed owners of retail businesses. Letters were sent to 120 owners of retail businesses listed in the Chamber's database requesting that they complete the brief survey and return it by mail. Reminders were sent two weeks later to those businesses that had not yet completed a survey. We received 26 completed surveys, a completion rate of 22 percent.

The survey contained seven items and was modeled after the community survey administered to private citizens reported in Chapter Two. Each item contained four response options: very positive, somewhat positive, somewhat negative, and very negative. For example, responses to a question about how good a job the DPD was doing fighting crime included "a very good job," "a somewhat good job," "a somewhat bad job," and "a very bad job." The seven questions were

- How good a job is the DPD doing fighting crime?
- How promptly does the DPD respond to calls from business owners?
- How helpful is the DPD toward victims of crime?
- How well does the DPD work with business owners to solve local problems?
- How well does the DPD work with business owners to prevent crimes?
- How satisfied are you with police presence in your neighborhood?
- How effective is the DPD in dealing with problems that concern business owners?

Figure 5.1 presents the percentage of positive responses for each survey item. The first thing to note about the figure is that the responses by retail business owners are considerably less positive than are the responses of private citizens reported in Chapter Two. Responses to

Figure 5.1
Business Owners' Opinions of Police

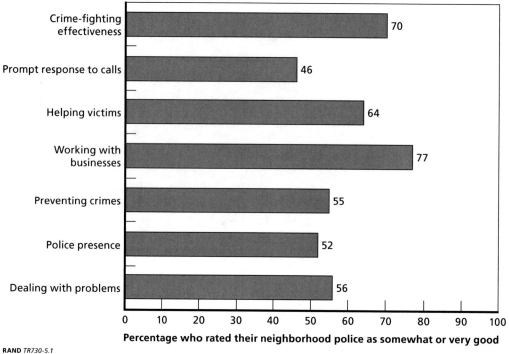

Percentage who rated their neighborhood police as somewhat or very good

RAND *TR730-5.1*

items in the community survey ran about 80 percent positive. In contrast, not a single item in the business survey attained an 80 percent positive rating, and most of the items achieved only slightly better than a 50 percent positive rating. The other noteworthy thing about the figure is that the ratings vary substantially from one item to the next. While the DPD received high marks (77 percent positive) for working with business owners to solve local problems, less than half of respondents (46 percent) gave favorable ratings to promptness of response to calls for service from businesses, and only a bare majority (52 percent) gave the DPD satisfactory ratings for police presence in their neighborhood.

We conducted identical surveys in two other jurisdictions, and compiled the results from the seven questions into a composite favorability score ranging from 1 to 4. Figure 5.2 compares the results for Dallas with the other two survey sites. While the ratings for each of the three sites were in the positive range, ratings for Dallas were somewhat lower than for the other two sites. Since the numbers of surveys in each of the sites was small, findings must be regarded as tentative.

Conclusion

Satisfaction of Dallas business owners with police services were in the same range as responses of business owners of two other municipalities, but noticeably lower than satisfaction of the public at large. However, small numbers argue against drawing sharp conclusions. In subsequent surveys, we will seek to increase the numbers of retail business responses and explore the reasons why satisfaction may be lower among this segment of the public.

Figure 5.2
Business Owners' Opinions of Police: Comparison of Dallas with Other Municipalities

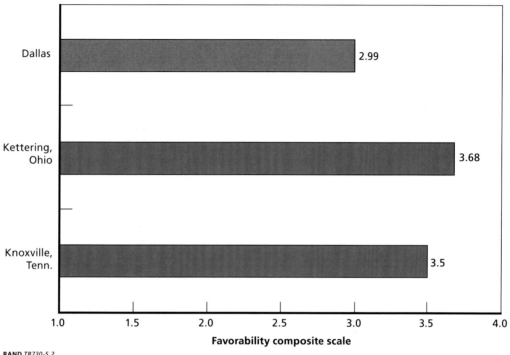

CHAPTER SIX

Conclusions

The surveys conducted in 2008–2009 will act as a benchmark against which to assess changes that occur in the DPD as a result of Caruth Police Institute staff development and problem-solving initiatives. These initial surveys also serve as a snapshot of the DPD today.

Community Survey

The community survey results show that the public generally holds positive opinions about the DPD in terms of effectiveness, professionalism, fairness, and management. On most measures of effectiveness, fairness, and management, roughly 80 percent of residents surveyed responded positively. The two items with the least number of positive responses were promptness of response and dealing with citizens without bias. But, even on these items, two-thirds of respondents registered positive responses. On items assessing police professionalism, the response was also largely positive. The DPD received the greatest criticism in terms of stopping people without good reason. But again, even on this item, two-thirds of survey respondents did not think that such behavior was common.

We observed statistically significant differences in police effectiveness, police professionalism, and neighborhood problems according to division. However, we want to emphasize that, even though the analyses of division differences controlled for effects of age, race, and gender, the analyses do not necessarily demonstrate that differences between divisions are the result of police-citizen interactions, police leadership, or other factors under the control of the DPD. It is entirely possible that the differences are due to other, unmeasured, differences between divisions, such as indicators of poverty, transience, or local media. The results do suggest that there are differences between divisions in opinions about police services, as a result of perceptions derived from conduct of the police, the media, or other sources. Regardless of whether the differences result from police behavior, the results provide reason to look further into the causes of why policing in some divisions is perceived more positively than others.

Dallas compared favorably to other municipalities where similar question sets have been used to assess opinions of the police. While such comparisons are questionable due to differences in survey methods, size of jurisdiction, population make-up, and changing times, the results presented here suggest that the DPD is perceived at least as positively as the police in other municipalities.

The fact that the baseline perceptions of police effectiveness and professionalism were so positive suggests that it would be useful to amend the scales to generate responses that leave room to see improvements that may happen in the DPD in upcoming years. We plan to make use of the new British community survey of opinions of the police to identify additional items that could be added to the Dallas survey. Future administrations of the survey also need to develop better ways to reach Dallas's Hispanic population and generally to produce samples that better mirror the Dallas population.

Contact Surveys

The responses of citizens who called upon law enforcement for assistance were very positive. Citizens who had received summonses were also generally positive in their evaluation of the encounter, although somewhat less so. There were no statistically significant differences between divisions on the voluntary contact surveys. This may result from the fact that officers in all divisions undergo the same training and are under the same central command. However, comparisons between Dallas and four other law enforcement agencies showed minimal differences as well. It is good news that citizens who have contact with the police are satisfied with the way the interaction was handled. However, these patterns suggest that the voluntary contact surveys need to be revised to generate a greater range of responses that will act to better differentiate divisions and agencies.

The involuntary contact survey results did show some differentiation between divisions and between Dallas and three other agencies.

Officer Survey

Dallas officers were mixed in their responses to items concerning job satisfaction. On some items (e.g., knowing what is expected of them), responses were very positive, but on a number of items (most notably, receiving praise for good work), less than a majority gave positive responses. Job satisfaction among Dallas officers was below that of the three other performance indicator sites, but the other sites are not comparable major city agencies.

The leadership perception questions produced bifurcated answers. A majority of officers held positive opinions about leadership provided by their immediate supervisors, but only small minorities held positive opinions of departmental leadership. This is an area where the Caruth Institute clearly can make a difference. The courses offered by the institute should enhance leadership skills among senior and intermediate level DPD administrators, and give officers and their immediate supervisors a better appreciation of the quality of leadership that resides in the DPD.

Integrity survey results suggest that Dallas officers have high ethical standards.

While we are pleased with the response to the survey, we will look for ways to increase completion rates in future administrations. We will involve ourselves in the process to a greater extent, explore better ways of introducing the survey, introduce more systematic follow-up on the initial invitation, and explore the idea of an incentive in the form of a lottery.

Retail Business Survey

Opinions of the police expressed by retail business owners were not as positive as those expressed by the community at large. Large majorities of business owners rated the police favorably in terms of working with business owners and crime-fighting effectiveness. However, less than a majority gave the DPD positive marks for response time.

The response to the business survey was good for a mailed survey. However, in the future, we plan to work with the Dallas Chamber of Commerce to send retail business survey invitations by email and allow completion on the Internet. This method of administration will be less expensive and should produce a higher response rate.

Community Survey Sampling Frame and Weighting Procedures

The sampling frame for the Dallas survey was based on stratified sampling of directory-listed numbers. The use of directory-listed numbers enabled precise pre-identification in which of the seven police divisions the respondent lived. While random sampling would have produced greater coverage of all households, it would have been impossible to pre-identify the police division, nor could respondents be relied on to correctly identify the police division within which they lived. In acquiring the sample, researchers identified the census block groups that make up each of the seven divisions. Listed numbers within each of the divisions were selected. The sample was purchased from Survey Sampling, Incorporated: Initial purchases were based on estimated compliance rates. Once acquired, the sample was loaded into a CATI system that controlled the number of attempts per household until the 150-completion–per-division target was reached. Up to six attempts were made to contact a household before it was removed from the working sample. (Attempts and rates are included in the accompanying table.) Any adult in the household who was contacted by the Schaefer Center survey staff was considered an eligible respondent for the purpose of this survey.

Survey work ran from June 25 through July 30, 2008. However, upon completing the initial target of 150, it was discovered that Hispanics were seriously undercounted in some divisions. The overall proposition of Hispanics in the initial sample was 8.7 percent. Undercounts of Hispanics could stem from a number of sources: language barriers, both real and feigned as a way of refusing; greater reluctance to answer questions about the police; lower probability of directory listed; and, greater reliance on cell-phones.

To increase the number of Hispanics in the sample, an additional sample was purchased from lists that identified Hispanic surnames. The new sample was called though once allowing the Schaefer Center to complete all surveys for which language was not an issue. The remaining surveys were completed by Maryland Marketing, Inc., a local firm with greater Spanish-speaking resources. The final interview was completed on November 25, 2008. Table A.1 presents statistics on the three phases of the survey.

Table A.1
Community Survey Summary Statistics

	Original	Hispanic	Maryland Marketing
Sample size	13,650	2,994	5,280
Refusals	2,579	758	576
Nonworking numbers	4,000	917	950
Completions	1,037	77	248

The final sample contained 43 percent whites, 30 percent Hispanics, 24 percent blacks, and 3 percent Asian or other, compared with population figures of 31 percent white, 42 percent Hispanic, 23 percent black, and 4 percent Asian or other. Sample gender distribution was 38 percent male and 62 percent female, compared with a population distribution of 51 percent male and 49 percent female. Sample age distribution included 19 percent age 18–35, 32 percent age 36–55, and 49 percent over 55, while the city population distribution for age included 39 percent age 18–35, 38 percent age 36–55, and 23 percent over 55.

To better reflect the population demographics of Dallas, the sample was weighted. Weighting is a commonly used technique with survey data to compensate for sampling error. In any survey, the demographics of the sample will differ to a greater or lesser extent from the demographics of the population. Weighting is used to adjust for demographic groups that are under- or overrepresented in the sample of people that completed the survey.

To weight the Dallas community sample, we used the 2005–2007 American Community Survey 3-Year Estimates for the City of Dallas, Texas (available on the Census Bureau's American FactFinder Web site [U.S. Census Bureau, 2009]), to ascertain the percentage of the population that is of the ages and genders shown in Table A.2. We used the same dataset to ascertain the city population breakdown by race/ethnicity (white, Hispanic, black, Asian, and other). First we divided the population percentage by the community percentage for age and gender. Then we did the same for race. We then multiplied the weight for race by the weight for age and gender.[1] Table A.2 shows the numbers used in the weighting process.

Table A.2
Weighting the Dallas Community Sample

Age	Gender	White	Hispanic	Black	Other
18–24	Male	1.489724835	3.026833997	2.06595365	2.757575758
	Female	1.755747126	3.567340067	2.43487395	3.25
25–34	Male	1.755747126	3.567340067	2.43487395	3.25
	Female	1.108892922	2.253056885	1.53781513	2.052631579
35–44	Male	1.309370738	2.660389203	1.8158382	2.423728814
	Female	0.846143193	1.719200032	1.17343323	1.56626506
45–59	Male	0.752463054	1.528860029	1.04351741	1.392857143
	Female	0.526724138	1.07020202	0.73046218	0.975
60+	Male	0.40967433	0.832379349	0.56813725	0.758333333
	Female	0.252625486	0.513286341	0.35034158	0.467625899

[1] This assumes that the distribution of age and gender is the same across the race/ethnic groups; we had no reason to suspect that this was a problem. We could not otherwise get specific percentages for each age-gender-race combination within the American Community Survey dataset, because of how information about race is recorded/reported.

Analysis of Covariance Results for Police Effectiveness, Police Professionalism, and Neighborhood Problem Scales

Tables B.1–B.3 show the results of the analyses of covariance that we conducted to isolate effects of division on effectiveness, professionalism, and neighborhood problem scales, holding constant the effects of age, race, and gender.

Table B.1
ANCOVA Model for Differences Between Divisions on Police Effectiveness Scale

Source	Type III Sum of Squares	Df	Mean Square	F	Sig.
Corrected model	137.043[a]	11	12.458	21.116	0.000
Intercept	665.190	1	665.190	1,127.429	0.000
Age	38.327	1	38.327	64.960	0.000
Male	3.364	1	3.364	5.702	0.017
Black	3.626	1	3.626	6.145	0.013
Hispanic	2.293	1	2.293	3.886	0.049
Other	0.002	1	0.002	0.003	0.956
Division	37.837	6	6.306	10.688	0.000
Error	784.118	1,329	0.590		
Total	15,914.640	1,341			
Corrected total	921.161	1,340			

[a] R squared = 0.149 (adjusted R squared = 0.142)

Table B.2
ANCOVA Model for Differences Between Divisions on Police Professionalism Scale

Source	Type III Sum of Squares	Df	Mean Square	F	Sig.
Corrected model	224.979[a]	11	20.453	22.226	0.000
Intercept	1,081.996	1	1,081.996	1,175.819	0.000
Age	35.414	1	35.414	38.485	0.000
Male	6.003	1	6.003	6.524	0.011
Black	40.245	1	40.245	43.735	0.000
Hispanic	40.810	1	40.810	44.348	0.000
Other	0.410	1	0.410	0.446	0.504
Division	18.443	6	3.074	3.340	0.003
Error	1,222.033	1,328	0.920		
Total	22,096.438	1,340			
Corrected total	1,447.012	1,339			

[a] R squared = 0.155 (adjusted R squared = 0.148)

Table B.3
ANCOVA Model for Differences Between Divisions on Neighborhood Problem Scale

Source	Type III Sum of Squares	df	Mean Square	F	Sig.
Corrected model	73.536[a]	11	6.685	17.121	0.000
Intercept	271.617	1	271.617	695.609	0.000
Age	0.027	1	0.027	0.068	0.794
Male	3.652	1	3.652	9.352	0.002
Black	.993	1	0.993	2.543	0.111
Hispanic	42.079	1	42.079	107.763	0.000
Other	2.319	1	2.319	5.939	0.015
Division	10.463	6	1.744	4.466	0.000
Error	518.940	1,329	0.390		
Total	5,979.167	1,341			
Corrected total	592.476	1,340			

[a] R Squared = 0.124 (adjusted R squared = 0.117)

References

Avolio, Bruce J., and Bass, Bernard M., "Multifactor Leadership Questionnaire," 3rd ed., Menlo Park, Calif.: Mind Garden, 2008.

Bureau of Justice Statistics, *Contacts Between Police and the Public: Findings from the 2002 National Survey.* Washington, D.C.: U.S. Department of Justice, 2002.

Klockars, Carl B., Sanja Kutnjak Ivkovich, William E. Harver, and Maria R. Haberfeld, "The Measurement of Police Integrity," *National Institute of Justice Research in Brief*, May 2000.

Miller, Joel, and Robert C. Davis, "Unpacking Public Attitudes to the Police: Contrasting Perceptions of Misconduct with Traditional Measures of Satisfaction," *International Journal of Police Science and Management*, Vol. 10, No. 1, March 2008, pp. 9–22.

Reisig, Michael D., and Roger B. Parks, "Experience, Quality of Life, and Neighborhood Context: A Hierarchical Analysis of Satisfaction with the Police," *Justice Quarterly*, Vol. 17, No. 3, September 2000, pp. 607–629.

Skogan, Wesley G., "Citizen Satisfaction with Police Encounters," *Police Quarterly*, Vol. 8, No. 3, 2005, pp. 298–321.

Thackery, John, "Feedback for Real," *Gallup Management Journal*, March 15, 2001. As of September 9, 2009: http://gmj.gallup.com/content/811/Feedback-Real.aspx

U.S. Census Bureau, American FactFinder, Web site, 2009. As of September 10, 2009: http://factfinder.census.gov

Vera Institute of Justice and the Lieberman Research Group, *Neighborhood Satisfaction Survey: Final Report*, New York: Vera Institute of Justice, 2003.